a scrupulous meanness
and other poems

shyamal bagchee

BuschekBooks

Copyright © 2004 shayamal bagchee
All rights reserved.

Library and Archives Canada Cataloguing in Publication

Bagchee, Shyamal, 1945-
    A scrupulous meanness and other poems / Shyamal Bagchee.

ISBN 1-894543-25-4

    I. Title.

PS8603.A44S37 2004   C811'.6   C2004-906423-1

Cover image:

R.B. Kitaj
If Not, Not (detail)
© Scottish National Gallery of Modern Art

Printed in Canada by Hignell Book Printing, Winnipeg, Manitoba.

BuschekBooks gratefully acknowledges the support of the Canada Council for the Arts for its publishing program.

BuschekBooks
P.O. Box 74053, 5 Beechwood Avenue
Ottawa, Ontario K1M 2H9
Canada
Email: buschek.books@sympatico.ca

Canada Council for the Arts   Conseil des Arts du Canada

"I HAVE WRITTEN IT FOR THE MOST PART IN A STYLE OF SCRUPULOUS MEANNESS," JAMES JOYCE (1906)

early versions of some of the poems in this book first appeared in these journals:

Canada: *ARIEL: A Review of International English Literature*, *Secrets from the Orange Couch*, *The Toronto Review*;

India: *The Commonwealth Review*, *Journal of the Poetry Society of India*;

Singapore: *World Literature Written in English*;

U.S.A.: *Café in Space: The Anais Nin Literary Journal*, *New Press Literary Quarterly*, *Sevenoaks Journal*, *South Dakota Review*;

E-zine: *nasty.cx*

This little book is dedicated to the loving memory of Bapin and Baba, and it is offered with love and *pronam* to Ma and Mamoni.

fore-verse

danse russe

—with apologies to William Carlos Williams

he, fifty some,
(no happy genius of his household)
performing awkward ballet
does strange study of geography
in front of bathroom mirrors

what he easily had
not such a long while ago
taut skin supple joints
he must now discover
by fitful ocular proof

locate through careful scrutiny
stretches of firm sinew
in the lower calves
by spying recover some smoothness
in few inches of dorsal muscle
or a reminiscent inward slope
above the buttocks
and such other scattered debris
of imploded youth
incongruously carried around
on papery-soled feet

the sixth season

the sixth season

and so begins the metaphysics
of loss
              begins
when you hear it
       with chitinous earlobes
       lax eyelids and
       a scrotum weighed down
       by its own redundance

begins?
they ask uncomprehending—

begins for you and me
never having heeded its flapping
in the last redwinged blackbird
of late fall in the immodest canola fields of spring
hotly negotiating green and yellow possibilities
in the heat of summer the tape
peeling off cracked windows
of ukrainian sausage store
in the stubborn mountain-ash berries
blackening in january sun
floating away from us
debris swept away
        by gusty monsoon

violet hours

profligacy of the orotund sun
moody gold   orange
salmon glory glory pink

in a bit
the bay settles down
nicely enough   dusty blue
      scummy grey uncertain black
      dusty darkish grey

and then comes the hour of anchors
of nets   of nets and hooks   and
fabulous fishing—

so,
you raised a drowned body
right?
now's the time for scratching
barnacles off blue toes
puffy cuticles curling away
peel the dermis—poke epidermis
strip off sodden sinews
looking for veins
for purple pearls   coagulated

also the violet
improbable inviolable tongue
swollen and heavy
with what it will not give away
      nor say why we mustn't fail to speak
      the little we think we might know
      very little perhaps

deep purple   and profligate

careless

    breathe!
        arise!
            rejoice!

but why should he care a whit
about the plucky honeysuckle
putting out pink on a limb
its invoice mailed out
the shrubbery yet to begin greening

any more than for the tawny powerwalker
her hips thrust this way and that
pale hair thrown to the wind

      NO MATTER THAT THEY'VE
      REPAVED THE ROAD TO SPRING
      HIS SUNDAY IS NOT SUMMERY ANY MORE

let them discourse
on their cellulars all they want;
trapped between black cadillac
and shrieking ambulance
this time he is not
ready for renovation

wintering

suppose merely that
she had come in from the cold

what if we grant only this
and just suppose that
she really *had* done that
and that summer was not
never again to be
no matter what
and that she was not lying
being, say, beyond the pale of fibs

at what tangent would we then
if any choice was ours
should or must we
place that fact
one fact that
so neatly
entirely
curved past
went around
circumscribed
without touching
our sense of it all
not altering it one bit
no matter how thin we sliced?

so, suppose for one millisecond
that we did, indeed, hear the truth
that it couldn't be milled down any finer

the invariably unprevaricating bitch
just suppose

suppose THAT

heavy hour blues

— i —

it is about time
he lined up his prejudices
behind a one-way window
and asked old acquaintances
to pick out any still identifiable

yellow leaves few or more

– ii –

cheering on his lagging
libido to catch up
to a silvery desire
his life now parodies itself

the incongruence
of coasting down one slope
and groaning up another—
all at once.

– iii –

no simple matter this—
she of easy virtue
he of none
take it easy fella

couple compatible
in more ways
than one
easy does it best

— iv —

her obstinate beauty
forever getting in the way

irritating

like a carelessly parked car
prevents easy berth
and hinders quick escape

— v —

and when she asked, sounding rather miffed,
why, if he was all that middle-agey,
his hair was still so black

seeing that a thinning pate settles nothing
he grew a grey beard just to assert
he had taken each day's buffeting on the chin

— vi —

this morning
the snow is only in ditches
dirtladen, seasonworn
except
wherever it's melted
the inverted patches of sky
are resolutely blue

startling ellipses and dashes
on a dun landscape

the interior far

second adolescence

his thoughts uncertain,
desires relentless
and sinews not in peak form—
a second adolescence

he wishes his parents
were here somehow
and in their prime again:

he needs answers
to questions he neglected to ask
the first time around

being 49 at russell square

—for SB (1912-1991)

i have been here before
sometimes alone
or my wife with me
or we with our children;
but never before at age forty-nine
this unremarkable cuspy year
and all by myself

the place hasn't changed much
a scattering of oversized pigeons
abundant roses, degenerate
on straggly bushes
unkempt overall like my thoughts
this june mid-morning

time on my hand i wonder today
what could this place mean
to a teenager growing up in new delhi—
plenty, when recalled by his
father on winter evenings
the family gathered in the warm kitchen
(an intimacy so much desired
and so seldom achieved today
even in the severest alberta winter)
closeness spurring vulnerable memories:

at forty-nine he went to distant london
to round off an education
stubbornly acquired in orphaned youth
and with dry sandwich in hand
he sat often on a bench like this one
among the many roses
missing wife, two sons
a daughter barely five
—no telephone in his
shared mezzanine flat

nor among the modest furnishings
of his faraway home,
cut off
seeking hard to fare well
in his self-made career
(i call home twice a day
and they even faxed me once
in these four days of absence)

brushing ghee on hot chapattis
low voiced but trying to sound
casual, even self-mocking,
speaking of unspeakable loneliness
of a middle-aged man taken from
his home
(and i too was lonely then
scared of growing up relentlessly
with no one to check things out)

and as children play around me
today in russell square
my daughter's bright face
ringed by curls, my son's eyes
bright and tentative
come back to me
terribly clear, terribly dear
and i think i know
what children mean, and father too

the place hasn't changed much
or so i imagine,
that it had been the same place
some thirty-five years back

i fly back in two days;
three years ago
i cremated my father,
who once sat in this park

refugees

at the very rear
of the lone oriental gallery
past sarcophagi, jade vases
faded khorassan rugs
and ancient stone tablets

a small ante-room
painted stark white
holding four objects
as deracinate as himself:
shiva in chola bronze
dancing his eternal rhythm,
the bodhisattva as an angry falcon,
and two miniature paintings—
kangra and mughal styles

℘

at the other end of town
there's "jaipur palace,"
a curry shop
down a winding cobbled lane
run by a retired rajput taxman
from liverpool
now in the once moorish
town of toledo

driving through bihar in july

kites shrieking in the scabrous sky
liaise hotly with wind battered
brown seared fringes of date-palm

and the naked dark child
who toddles across the red soiled
rutted road you cautiously
drive along
                leaves a scar
unlikely to heal for a long while
no matter how soon the broken
axle is fixed or clouds burst

so you turn your face swiftly
moving the gaze to hyacinth-choked
green ponds and wonder who scolded

thus far and no farther

there
are no thirteen ways
once high winter places
have done their thing
to you

then
you want only this
to have happened—
only in a dusty valley
beside fields
that are like
grey quilts

(or
is it the other
way around?)

out of sight of
sneaking coyotes
earshot of
lamenting loons

℘

the river bends
in midday heat,
on the boat tethered
under dull bodhi-tree
flies buzz a dead
boatman (merely
asleep?) naked
in the shadow
where the buck
finally stops

one way mirrors

home truths

the bump on the forehead
we did not particularly want
stays with us a long time
for all to see

and
there are usually big gaps
between ripping and stitching

and
when (as is mostly the case)
all sap is used up in mending
little remains for new buds

and love—
which is never in the beholder's eye—
makes short work of beauty

        smell the grass, i say

anniversary

the list of
the next to go
daily lengthens
several needs
dispensed with
each conceivable
convenient excuse

        least inconvenience
        generates more
        unregretted goodbyes
        waved casually
        at whatever
        one can now
        do without
        dispensable
        like habituated
        if and when
        coupling in the night

                the seven year itch
                still attested to
                live nerves—
                at twenty-five
                it's metallic silver
                electroplated in some
                taiwan of the mind

in fine

none of her acts slapdash
she cracks each egg in the middle
methodically with a rap
against the sharp edge
under the kitchen counter
fitting each narrow half shell
neatly into the broader half
she swiftly marches
on firm feet and clean shaven legs
to the gleaming garbage bin
across a shiny floor

when at last
she has to discard
ovaries, fibroids
and bit of this and that
she insists on a fine incision
aligned with the faint crease
just above the hairline

veracity

being much read in that kind of stuff
the large truths mainly leave me
distressed at my paltry performance,
nor look to me for the grand falsities
that make things really happen:
my impotence is all but open knowledge

so, i make do with the little ones
—of either kind—and having made
an art of them now discover
that i can hardly tell
where any difference lies

say, if we were to talk of love
i would surely have to admit
that the love of the woman who loves me
is still not all the love i need

> *hey, green river under my window*
> *give me your love today, right now*
> *don't just squander it on all and sundry,*
> *and don't ask for any in return*
> *for i am not the kind of fellow who*
> *feels sentimentally attached and so on*

on parting

        tenured fast
        in separation

        stations destined apart
        hand in hand
        part of the way
        ways part
        wherever

        ever so
        separate destinations
        it only seems
        that the sun's
        trapped in the trees
        transfixed
        will not set

        and, even so

what if

what if
is as good a phrase as any
one might find for a start
lean and brittle as last year's
grass when the snow is gone
starving as a january coyote
and as full of desire

the space it does not fill
is vast nevertheless
no amount of strenuous prodding
with mighty weapons of lust or rage
gets one anywhere approximating
meaning or climax
one does not come any place
one simply does not come
in that gaping pit
not open for mining

looks like detumescence has a purpose

after all

a scrupulous meanness

october

this fall
the rain falls
on so many rusty
leaves on ground
fallen from
branches now bare
and dark
falls on roots
gone to sleep

in certain
circles
it is suggested
that things
might sprout
again soon
in this spare
season

false

dimness

it's not the fly's eye
that i covet—
400 pupils
do not magnify
a sunset by much

even in dim light
near-blinkered eyes
reveal more
than i care for
—and then some

        so, i say, as long as
        a stray bird sails past
        and i sense it,
        dimness is all

        seeing too much
        or too soon
        one may never
        stop flitting about
        nor settle down
        until fly-swatted—
        surely by then
        it's too late

every momentary savouring
of the occasional passion
needs some tarrying
but being all-eyes
one only flies

comfort food

clarified emptiness
of three AM
he sits in the front room
nearly dark
bowl of cereal in hand
comfort food
for a restless hour

one wretched driver
setting out early to work
swerves loneliness
tires crunching northern snow
lately fallen on streets rooftops
pavements and bare branches

and he
in the suffused gloom
of furnishings sofas bookshelves
spoons his surplus meal
into a mouth long unused
to speaking

yet the mind senses easter
lily stalks lengthening by millimetres
each passing minute

sometimes he calls this place
home

on things

        some things are needless,
        always have been;
        unglued from rancour
        terror or yearning.

        some things are nothing.
        most things.

        some things prove
        a bit more worthwhile,
        though seldom wholly reliable—
        hardly all that steady:
        crisp snow on fence tops
        and a wind blowing.
        compass needles, nonetheless,
        veering with your pulses
        and living.

        some things are necessary.
        few things.

b(l)ank slip

often these days
he catches himself
not stopping enough
for love
nor tarrying any
to taste the salt
of desire

flitting busily
with mercurial feet
from throat-
searing smoke
of rush-hour streets
to slave lake's
clear frigidity
always efficient
at the big tasks
and never an error
on bank slips

irremediably competent
he stands tall
at the teller's wicket
the pink one in hand
for deposits
and the green
for withdrawals

winter woods

things being the way they are
these days he likes best
walking the woods in winter:

summer's undergrowth dead,
no briars or roses—
all distractions of colour gone;
with autumn's refuse safely buried
underfoot,
sun comes down clear
through empty branches,
reflects off the snow below

a double clarity
one might say

in/spaces

in the spring
at the cusp of
middle age
with crisp urgency
he is aware
of so many
unlived spaces
numerous vacancies
which too
could have been him

spaces
not great mind you
nor all elegant or expensive
though a few seem
prime enough locations
corner lots and such
others fit for
opulent cemeteries

not in every case unsoiled
nor holding much hope
dank sometimes
sometimes just
nooks and crannies
nonetheless
spaces unused
for homes
not likely
to be built

with battery low
and frantic days nearly done
he humbly puzzles over
this luxury of excess
in a mortgaged season

slippery arrangement

on certain fall evenings
the fog pushes a grey sky into his face
and he is hardly sure anymore
of broad avenues now slick underfoot
—then perhaps it's the clink of china
through an open window
some flowers in a vase—
the balloting is swift and one-sided:
senses have it, and moods don't

for a bit again he is happy enough
with that slippery arrangement

wordless

        don't trust words anymore?
        any word? none?

        loose tongued, no foothold,
        foot loose over
        a slip of rock
        tongued into dark waters.
        slippery.

        love, speak the third wish,
        the bitter one. now.
        "genie, i set you free."

breathing exercises
or
song of the prickly pear

- i -

you have been conceived. take a deep bow.
remember in time all mothers get blotchy skin
and after a while fathers go who knows where
without so much as a goodbye.
still, the prickly pear (defying all odds) ripens to some sweetness.
so, take the bow
—now

℘

- ii -

the maharajah is on a caparisoned elephant.
howdah is shaded by velvet, swords are gilded.
sir thomas rowe bows deeply—
he has letters from the chief
james of england, once of scotland.
—perhaps of india, someday soon.
exhale slowly counting to nine

- iii -

prapancha, the late lamented professor matilal
has written, is verbal proliferation.
one time i met gayatri chakravorty
—spivak to devotees who battle against eurocentrism—
at a bus-stop in oxford. she was on a pilgrimage
to hear matilal discourse on his deathbed

some breaths are more precious than others

- iv -

isla del sol, birth place of gods
and the inca, rises above titicaca
looking out onto the altiplano
here only the vicuña find enough food;
but the narrow urubamba valley below
is kinder to tourists and blares pop songs

wondering where
the *shining path* might have led to,
we huff and puff to the top
of ollantaytambo

- v -

desert storms are prickly with sand
(but bombs were optional, afterthought).
lovers are sweaty but happy too. tires are
knobby but take you places with or without maps.
its hot today, and the single mother is at the civic
waterpark with her kids.
no entry fee needed.

now that you have met the world why evade *prapancha*?

- vi -

and don't ever forget that afternoon
in far-away new england
ignatow's barely audible words,
and a gold-rimmed ginsberg
adjusting wheezy microphone

best minds of america
even better near the end when howl
is elevated to whisper

- vii -

consecrated pemmican, medicine
circles, a creek called saulteaux
saskatoon berries by cypress hills

what mainly remains is a cry
where the buffaloes jumped
and jumped and jum ...

the last beastly breaths
dissolving into ether

- viii -

oh the pleasure
of "shade-grown" coffee sipped in
neon-lit shopping mall: imagine beans
growing among exotic birds bees and apes,
plumped under rain forest canopy
on some happy equatorial mountainside

inhale the eco-friendly aroma
and delight in your good deed for the week
—inhale

- *ix* -

weave words around words
for nothing else will do.
there is no silver lining around this gloomy vapour,
self-swirling and self-perpetuating.
look for no hard cash at this bank machine
that dispenses without asking for passwords;
here pin-codes hold little sway.
proliferate, proliferate—
but come softly

- X -

*oum
shantih*

℘

coda

the lightness of being

some nights
prompted by the moon
or perhaps not
his mind insists on explanations
of the day's many irritations

there simply aren't
he finds
enough hours
to get those
and some sleep

(it's probably only insomnia
many must have it)